AF581237

SMPL

Simon Horan

Inquiries may be sent to the author by email through the link at

www.SimonHoran.com

This book can be ordered through all bookstores and through eplatforms such as Amazon.

It is also available through the author at

www.SimonHoran.com

“Stupendously simple and fun!”

Valorie Fisher,

author and illustrator, “I Can Do It Myself”

I cannot draw.

Literally, yes, I can place a pen onto paper and create a recognizable image. But my talent stops there. Luckily, I like to draw, and I have realized that people still like unrealistic drawings; just look at Keith Haring. So I boldly soldier forth.

My favorite style is what I like to call "simple," using only uncomplicated lines to draw things. It's easy to pick up and anyone can do it. Really. I hope you like it.

My inspiration was an elephant. When I was younger, my mom got a book of opposites called *Elephant Elephant* by Francesco Pittau and Bernadette Gervais, to give to our little cousin. I was too old for that sort of thing, so obviously I read it.

The book used elephants to display the opposites. "High" was an elephant on a tower, "low" was in a hole, and so on. But the "simple" one caught my eye. The drawing used only six lines! Neat! I was inspired by it and invented a lot of other animals in the same style.

Please enjoy my drawings!

The Rules

I do not count dots as a line. But I am very strict about what counts as a dot.

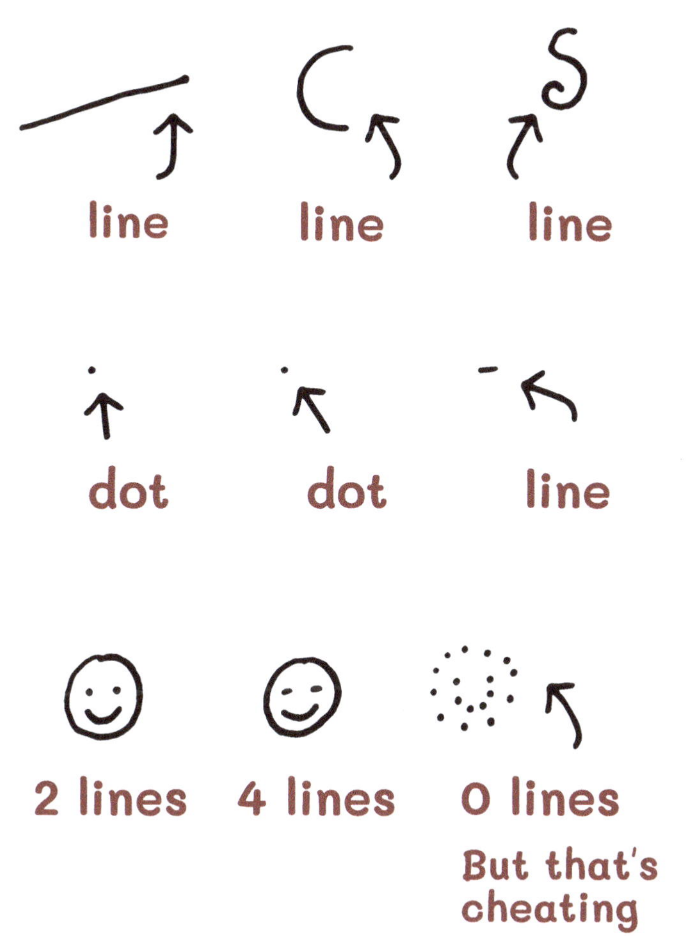

Dog

loyal friend animal

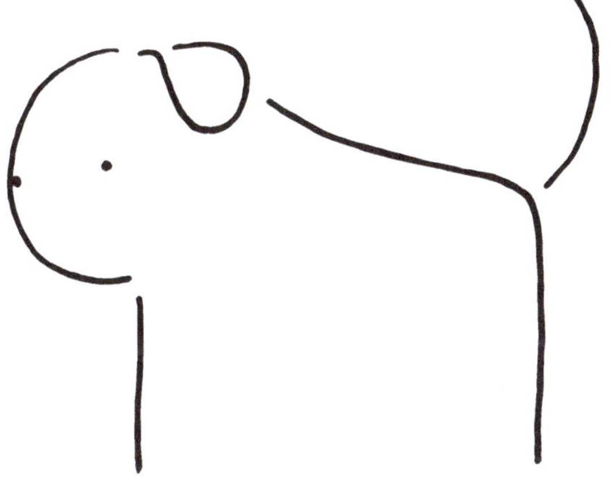

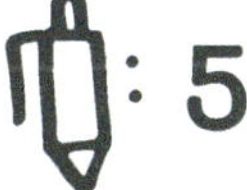
: 5

Cat

agile fickle pet

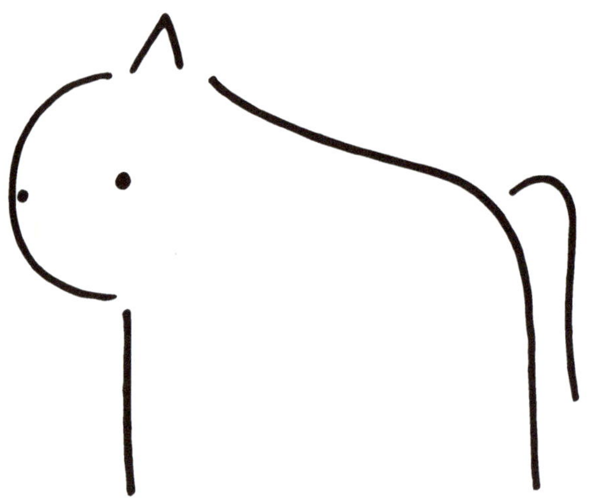

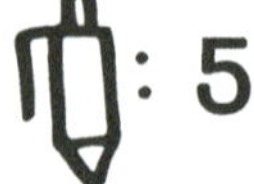

Horse

graceful riding animal

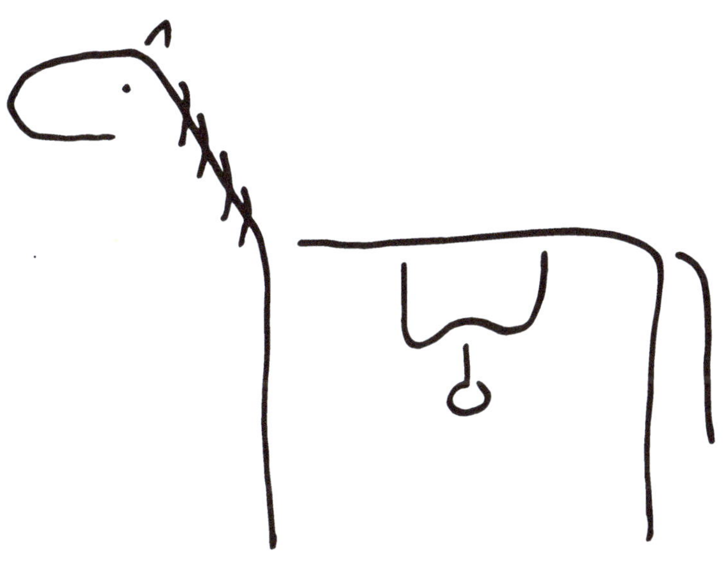

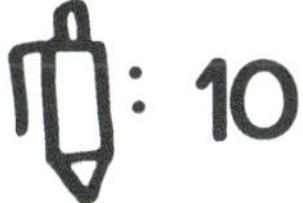

Deer

thinner wild horse

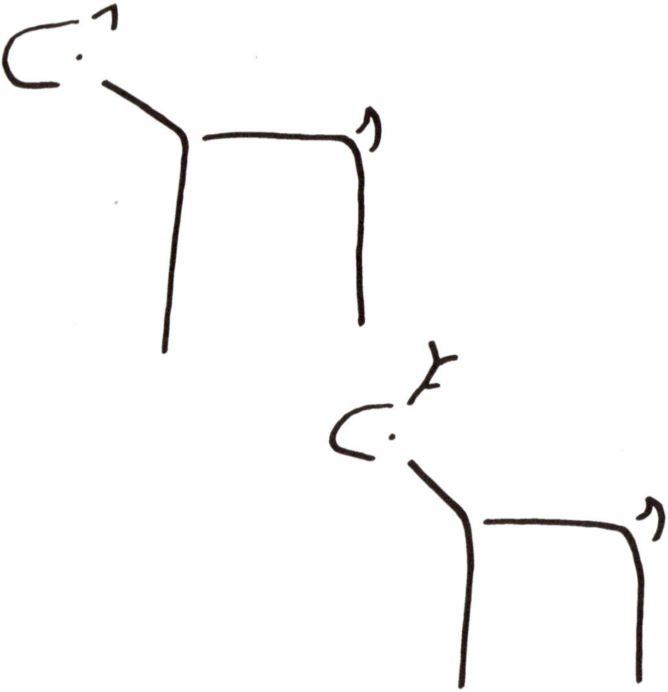

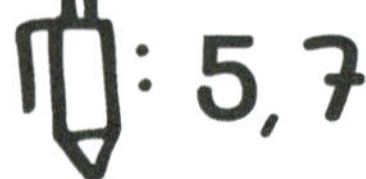

Cow

calm milk animal

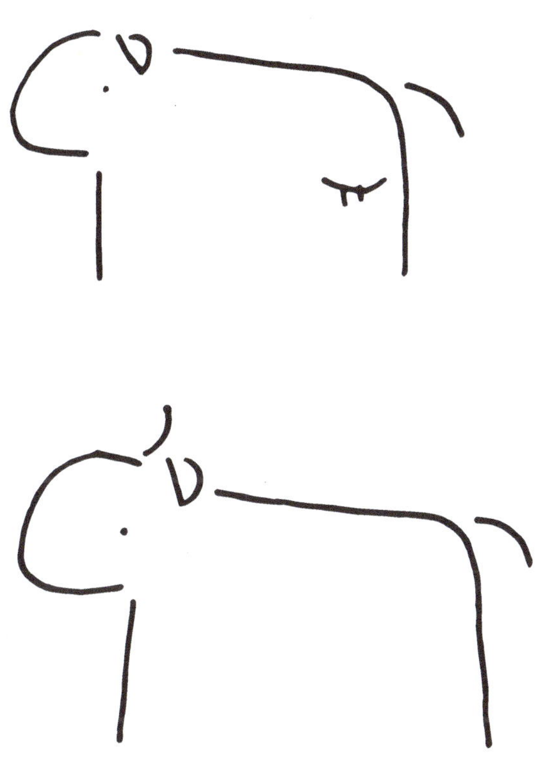

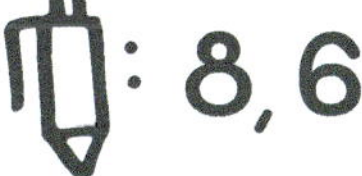

Pig

smart grunting animal

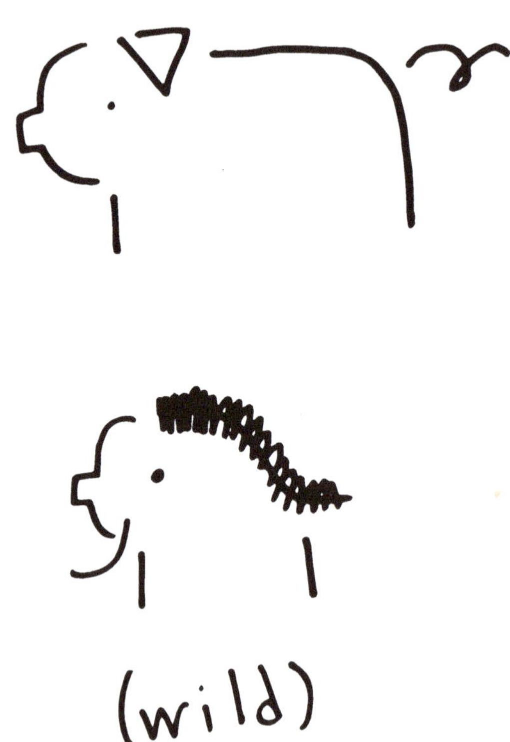

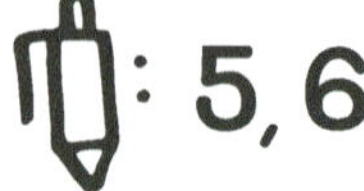

Various kinds of fish

Colorful swimming things

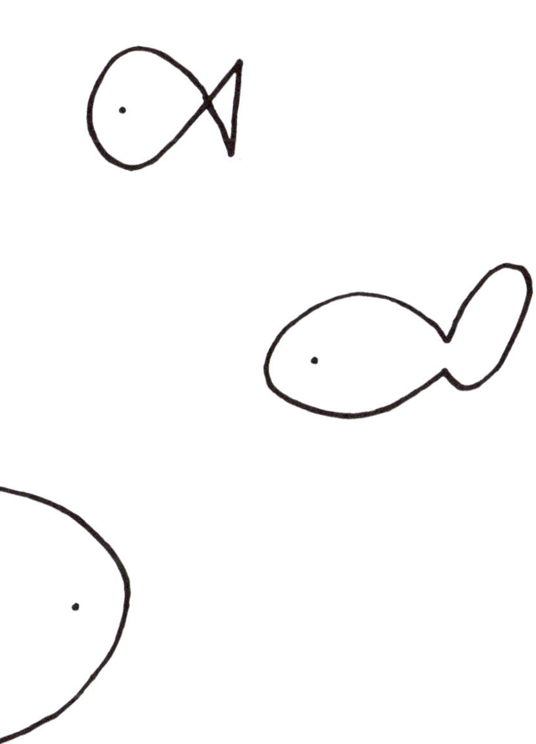

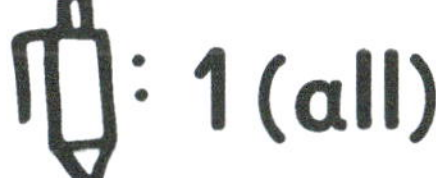

Frog/Toad

jumping rocklike animal

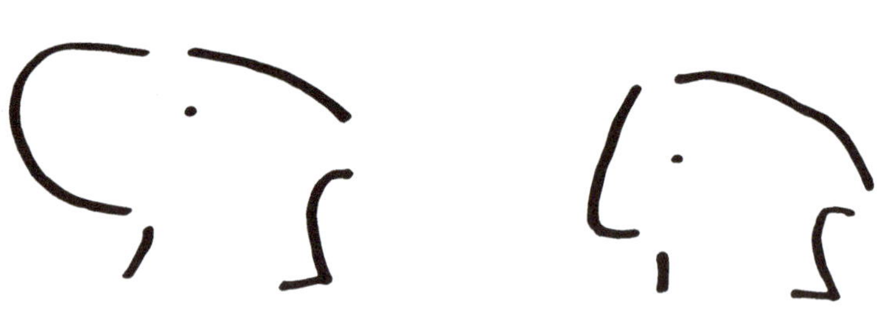

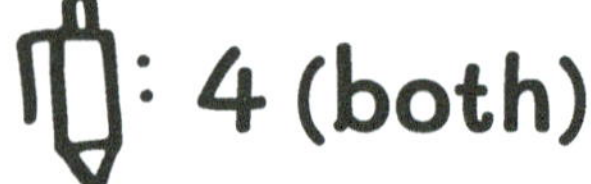

Bear

dangerous doglike animal

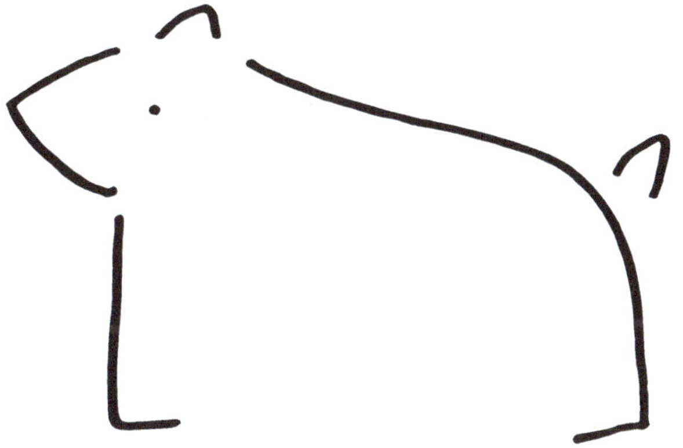

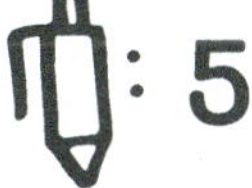

Snake

living rope thing

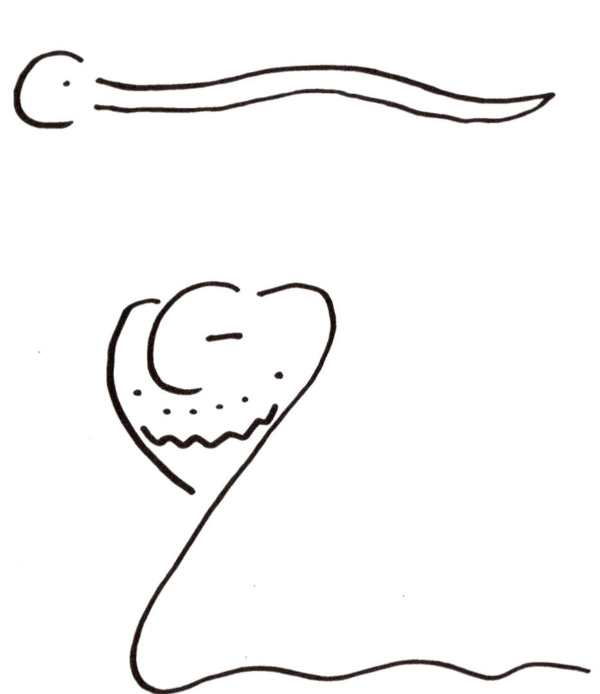

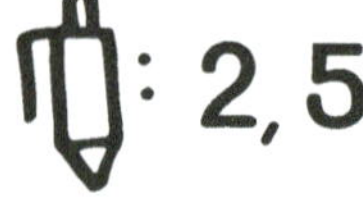

Zebra

horse with stripes

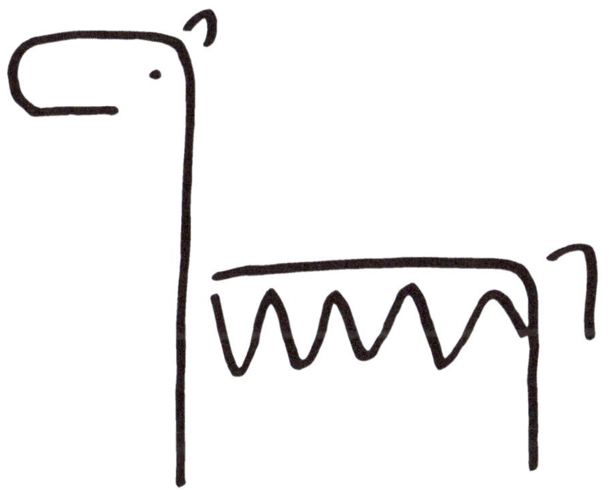

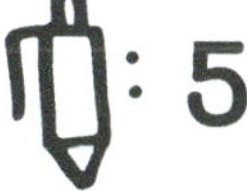

: 5

Rhinoceros

spike-nosed cow

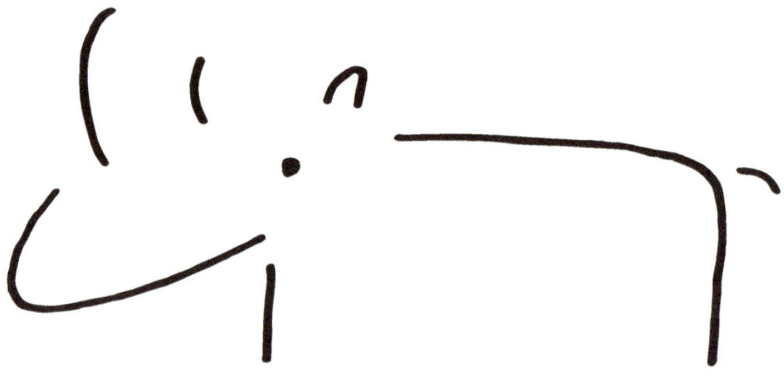

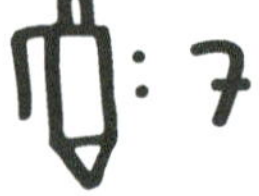

Hippopotamus

river cow

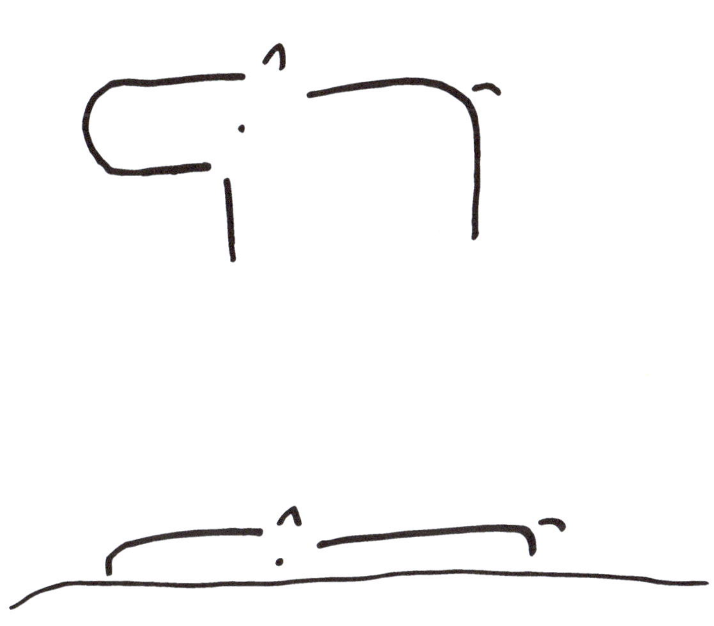

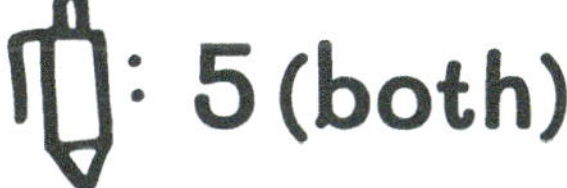

Giraffe

tall spotted deer

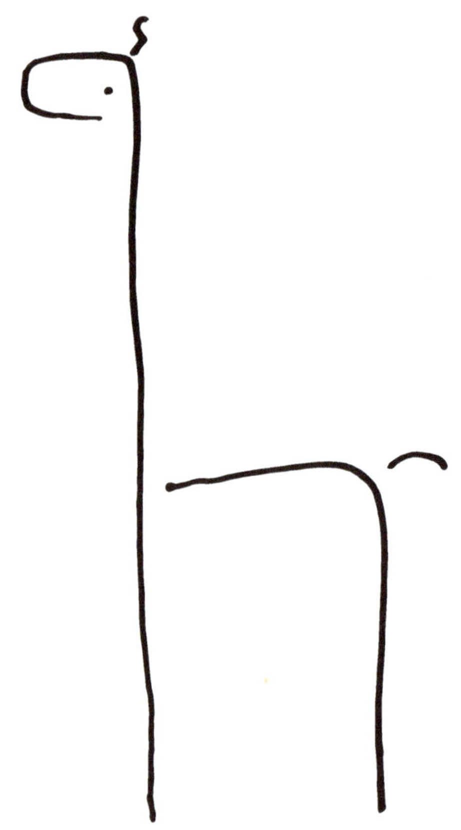

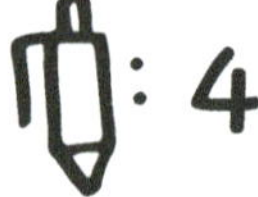

Elephant

huge long-nosed cow

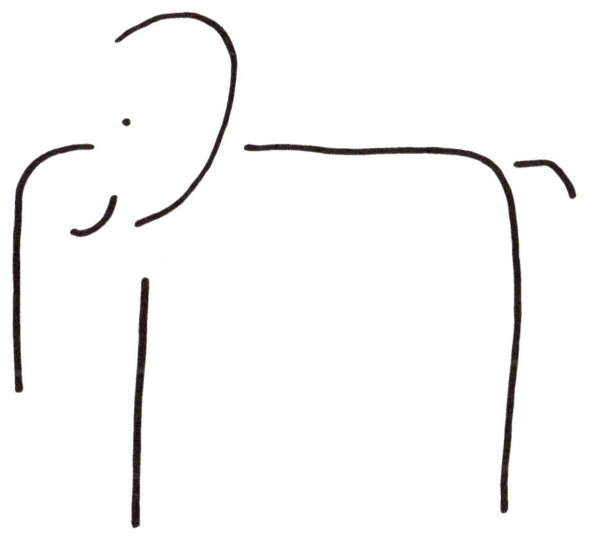

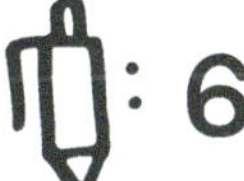

Lion

furry-necked cat

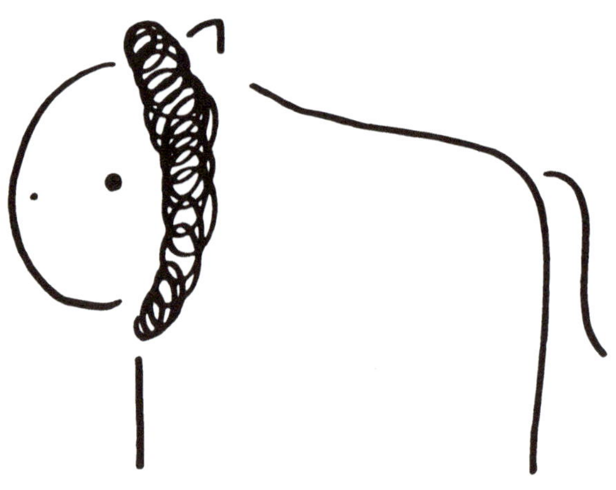

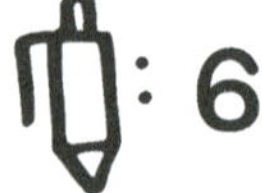

Tiger

striped cat

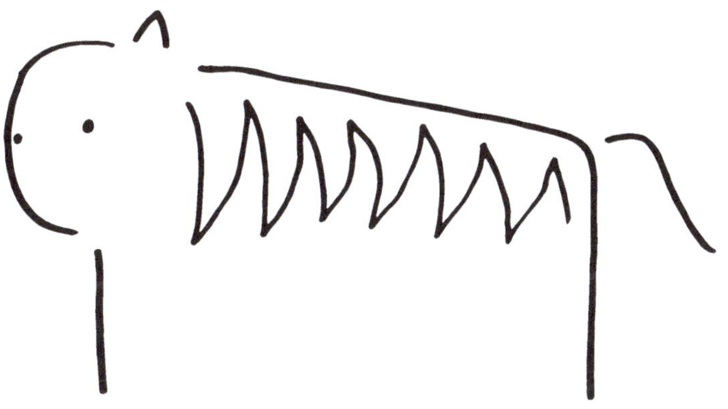

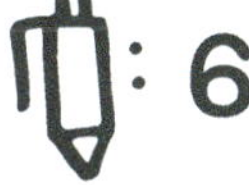

Cheetah

spotted cat

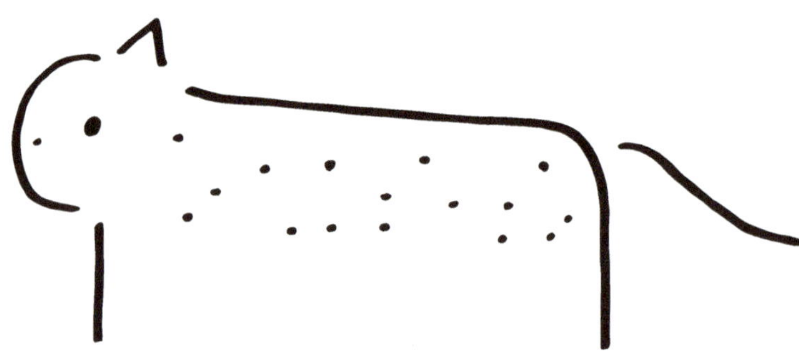

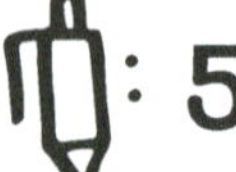

Monkey

hairy humanlike tailed animal

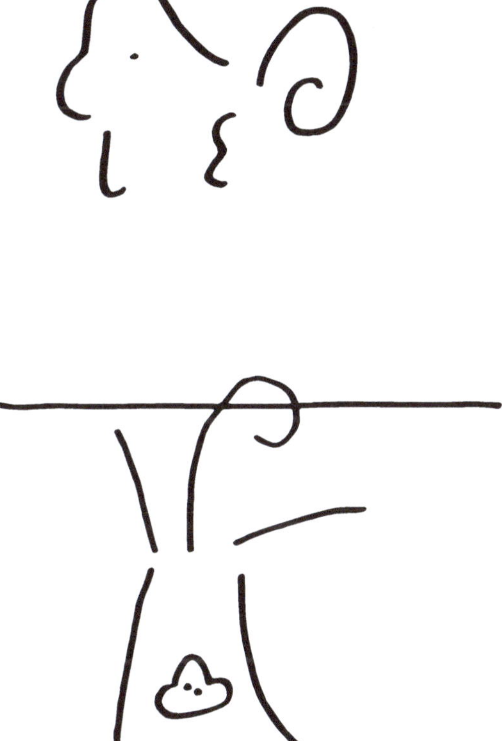

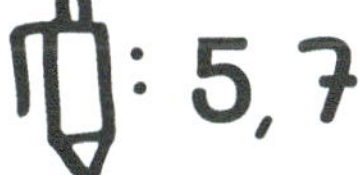

Gorilla

big tail-less monkey

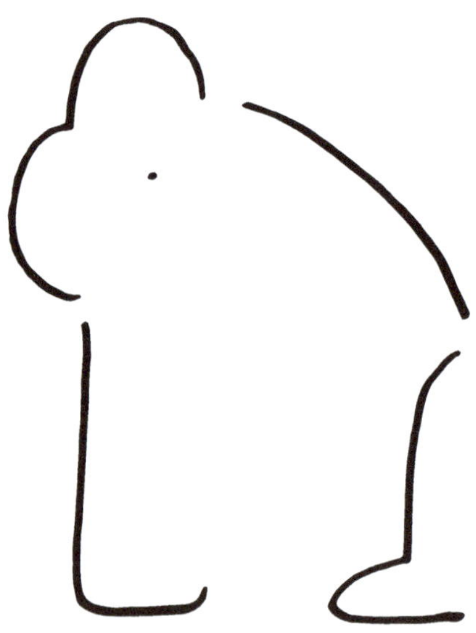

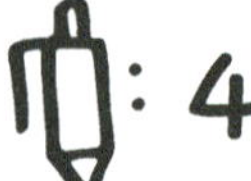

Alligator

living log with lots of teeth

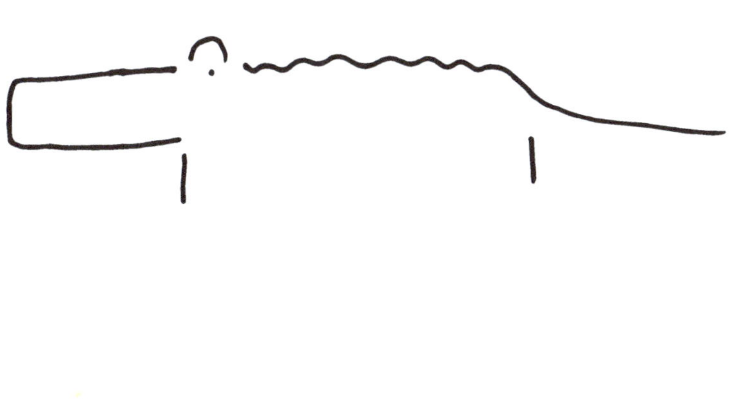

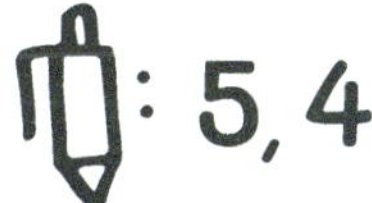

Dolphin

fishlike jumping water animal

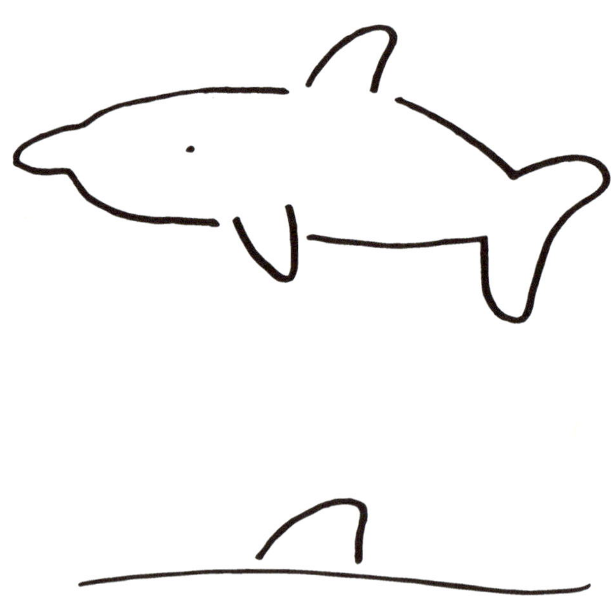

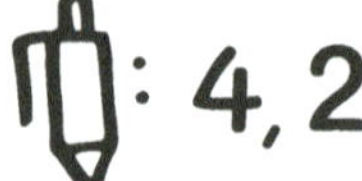: 4, 2

Shark

fast fish with sharp teeth

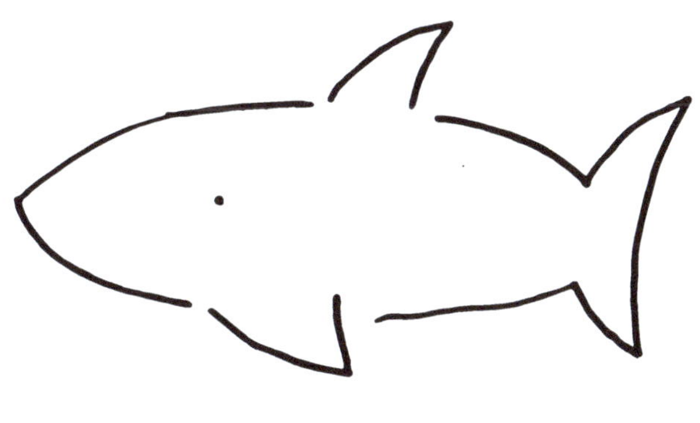

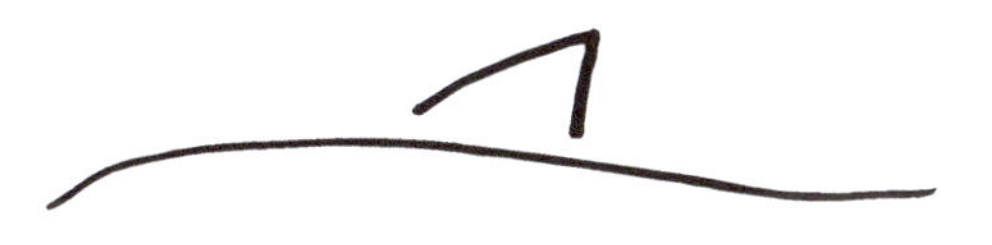

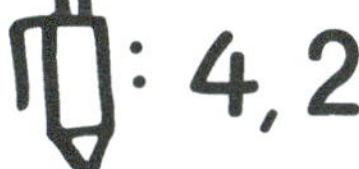

Seal

doglike fishlike animal

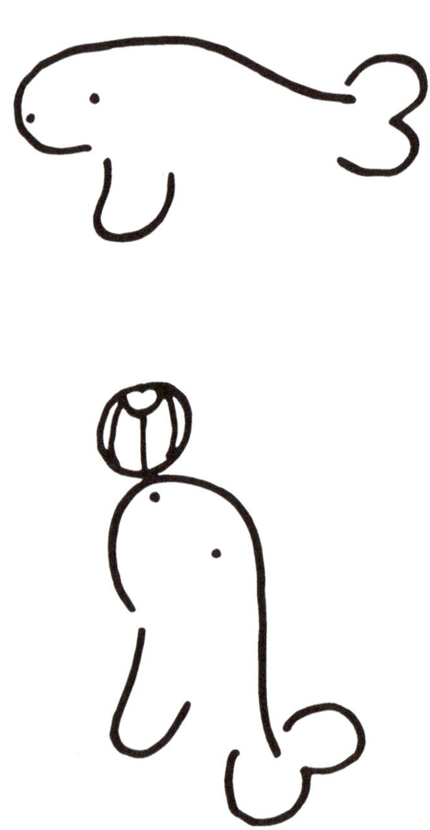

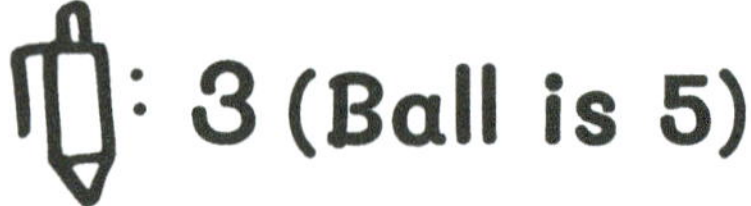

Urchin

rock with lots of spikes

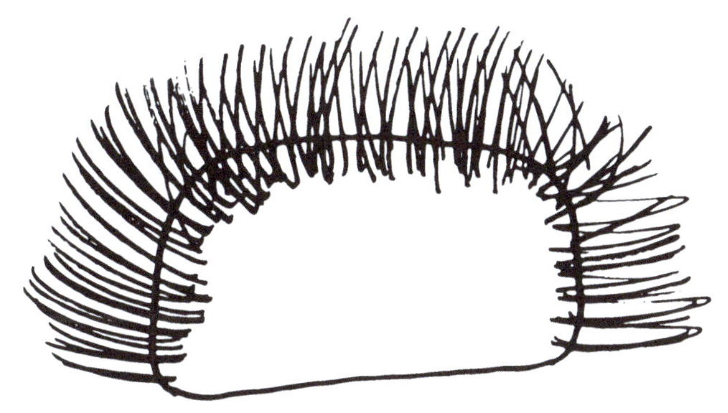

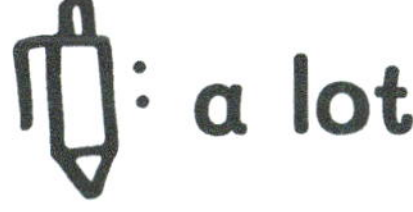

Stingray/Manta Ray

gliding fast fish

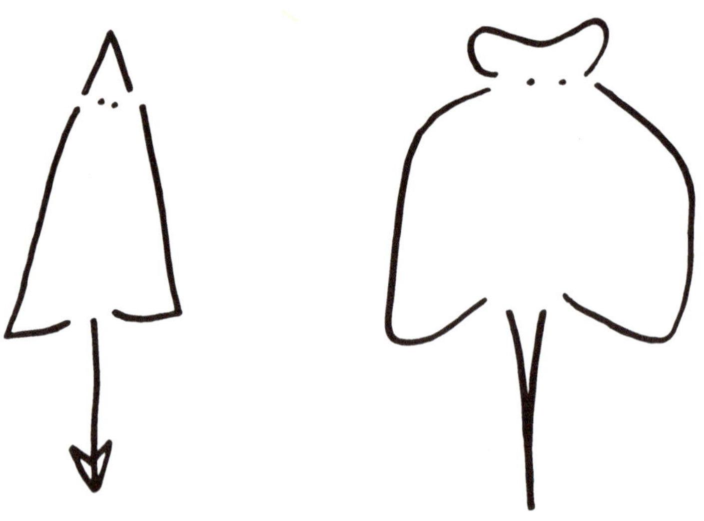

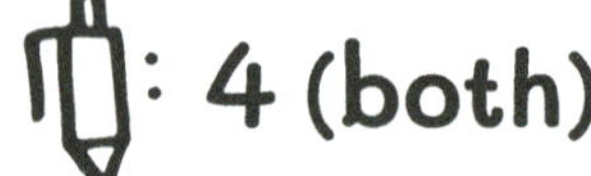

Manatee

giant seal

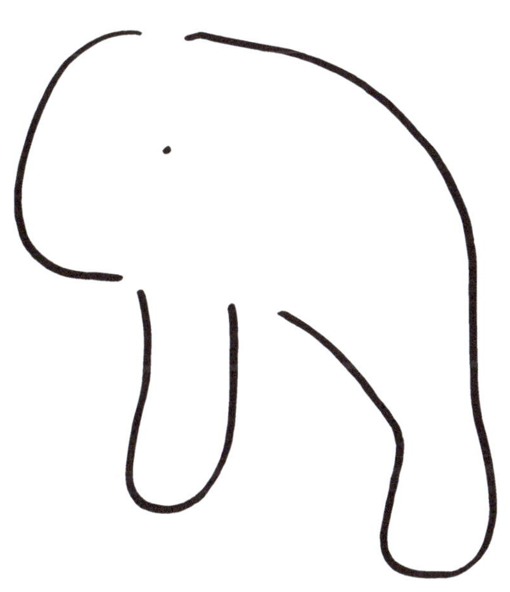

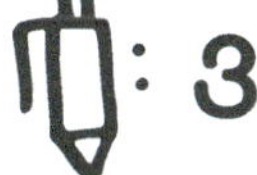

Whale

huge dolphin

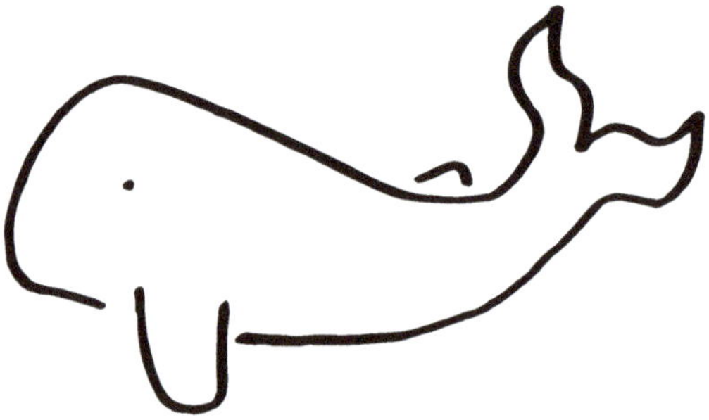

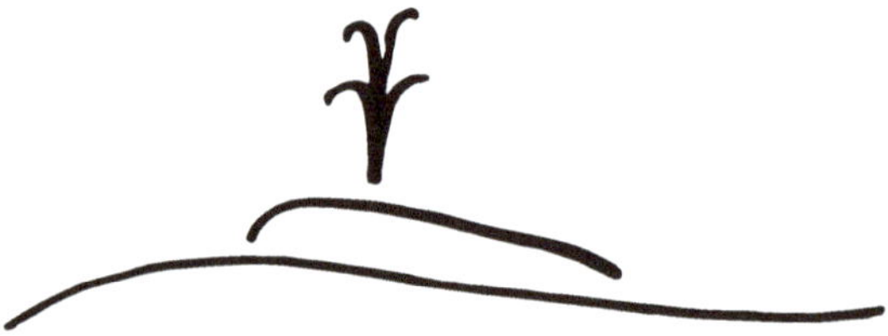

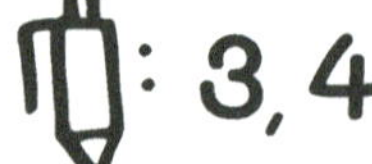

Narwhal

whale with a big horn

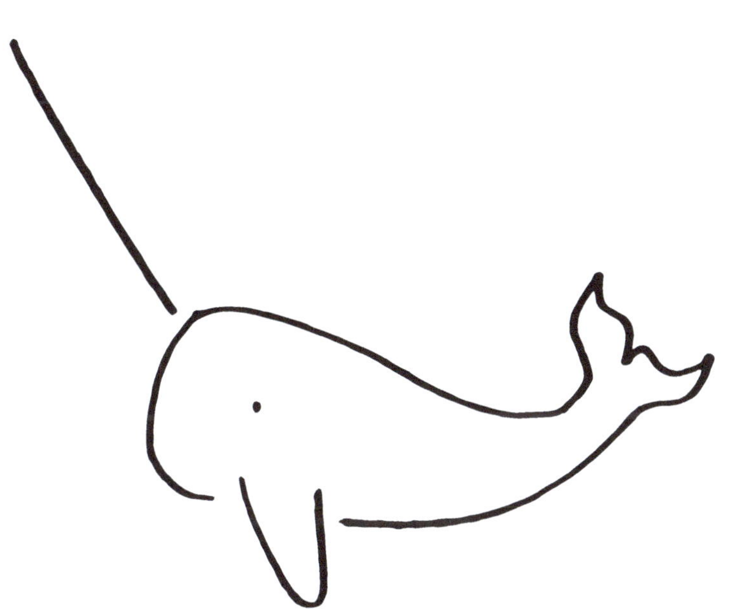

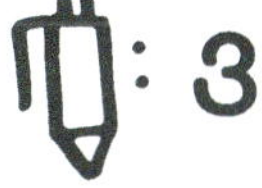

Octopus

pudding ball with lots of arms

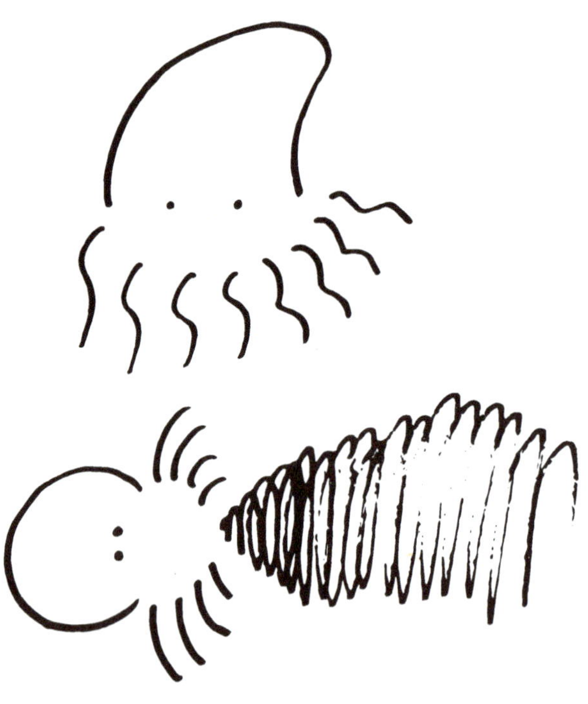

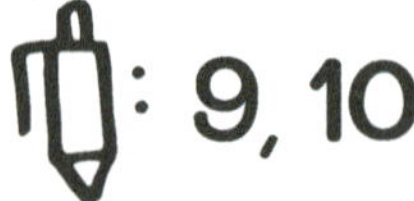

: 9, 10

Squid

long octopus

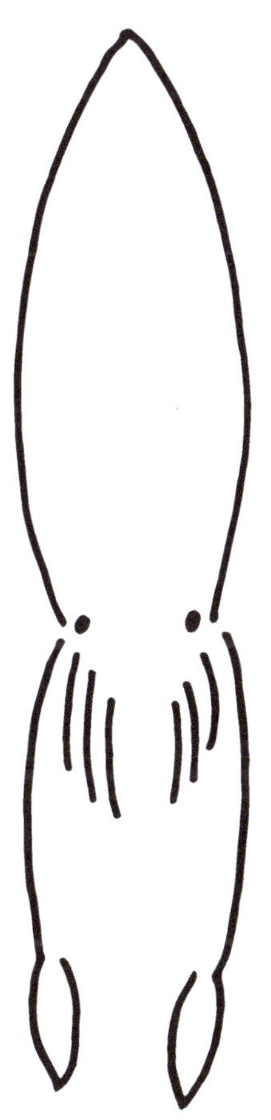

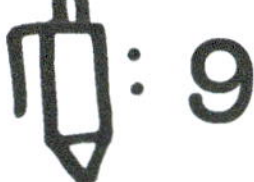

Eel

snakelike fish?

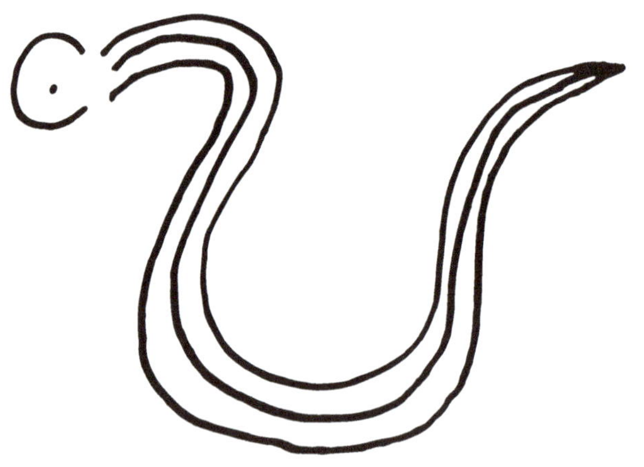

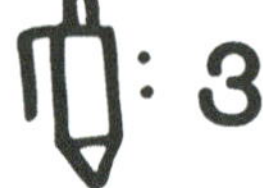

Sea Star

star-shaped rocklike thing

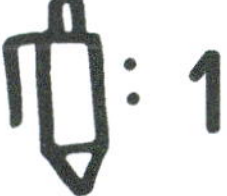
: 1

Nautilus

squid in a shell

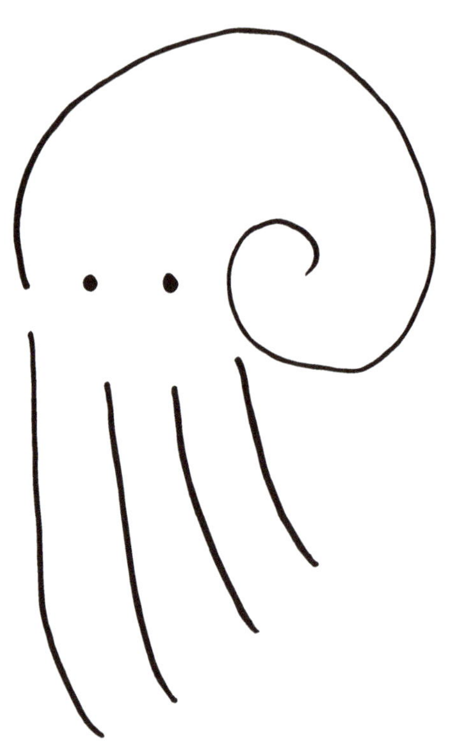

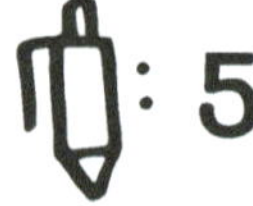

Jellyfish

blob with stinging strings

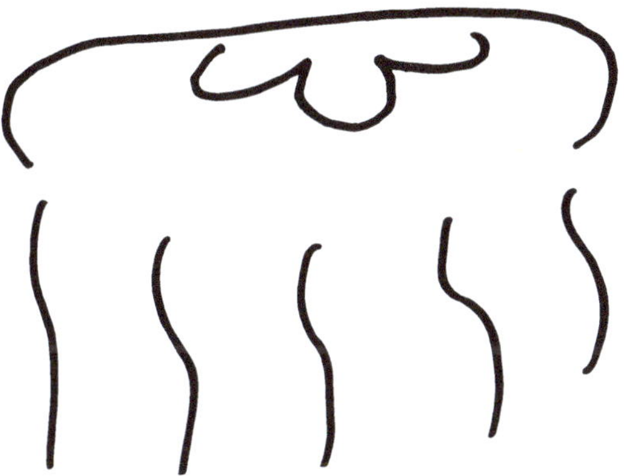

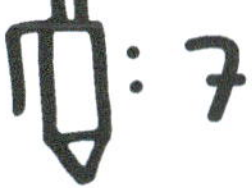

Turtle & Tortoise

slow walking rock

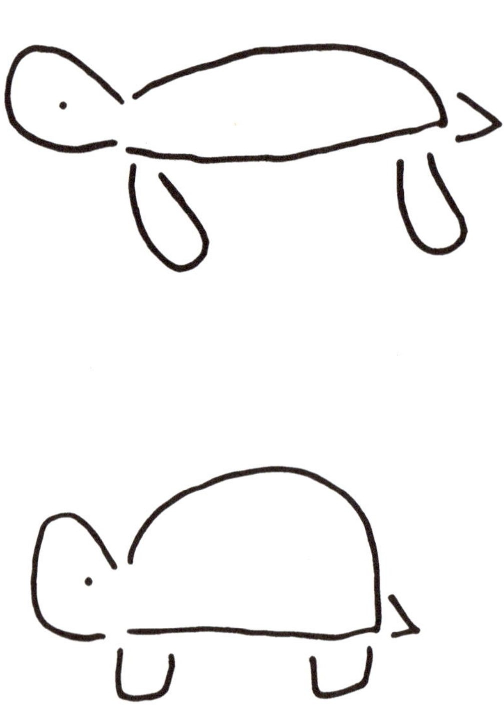

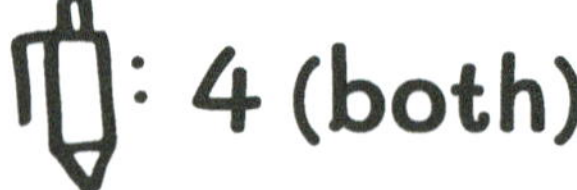

: 4 (both)

Crab & Lobster

underwater buglike
pinching things

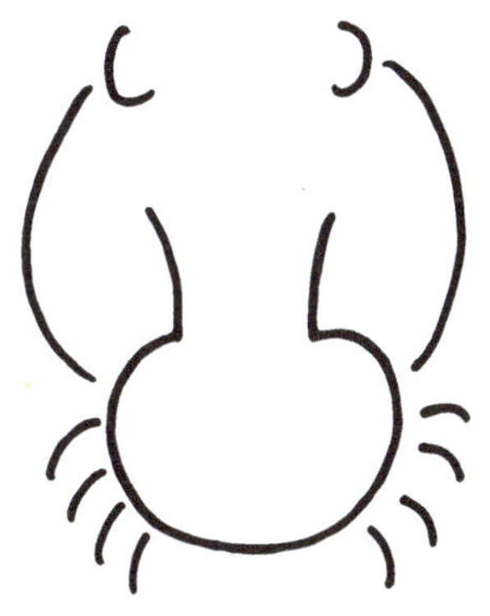

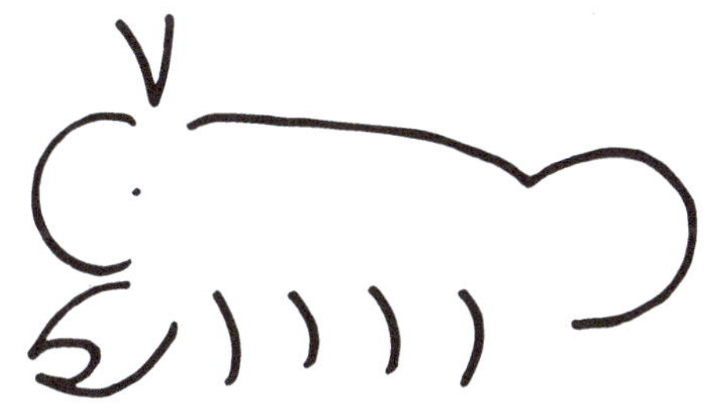

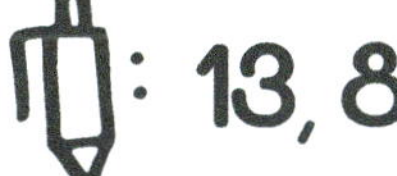

Mouse & Rat

small furry thief animals
"varmint"

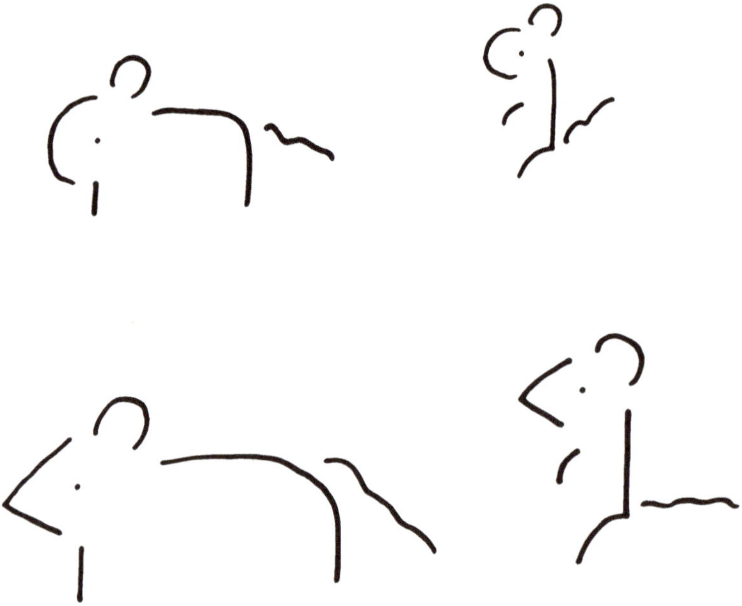

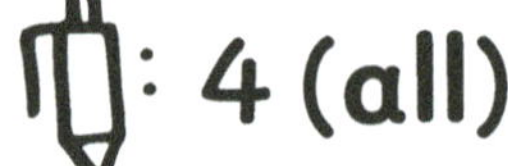

Rabbit

long-eared hopping mouse

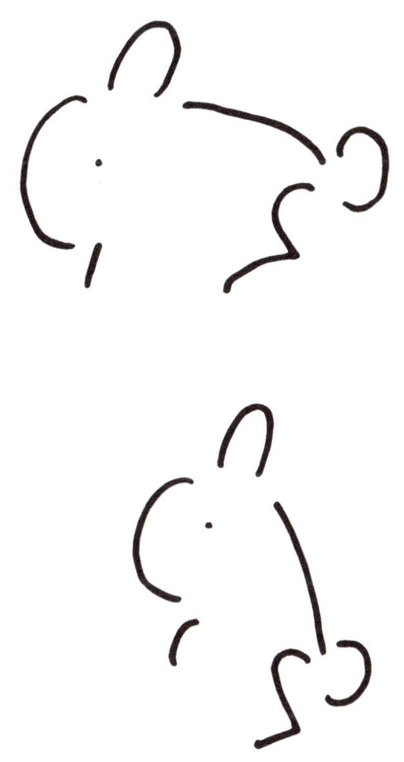

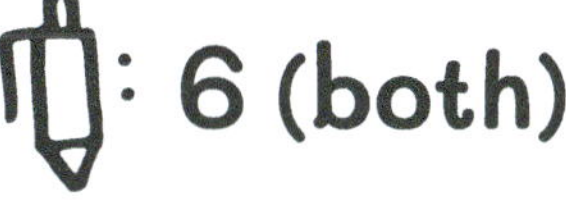
: 6 (both)

Squirrel

long-tailed tree mouse

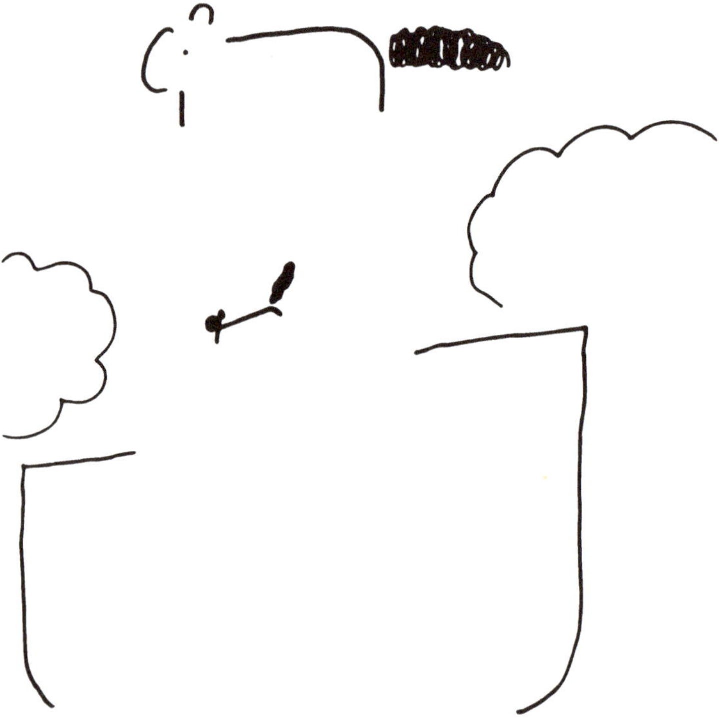

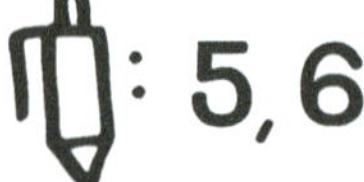

Hamster

fat, tail-less mouse

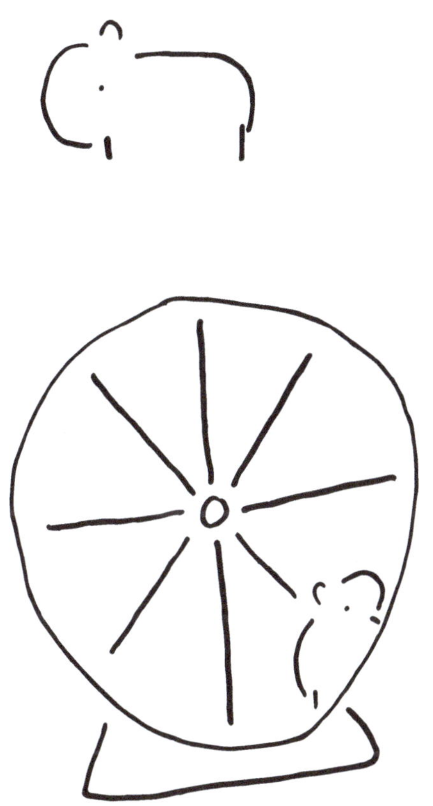

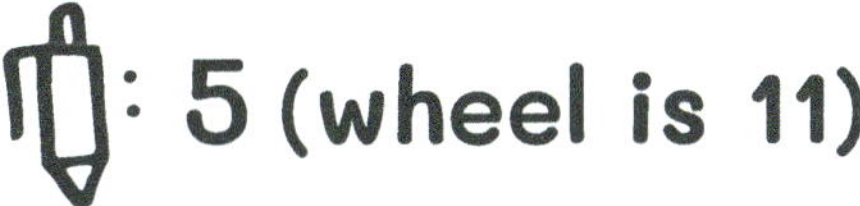

Chinchilla

big-tailed hamster

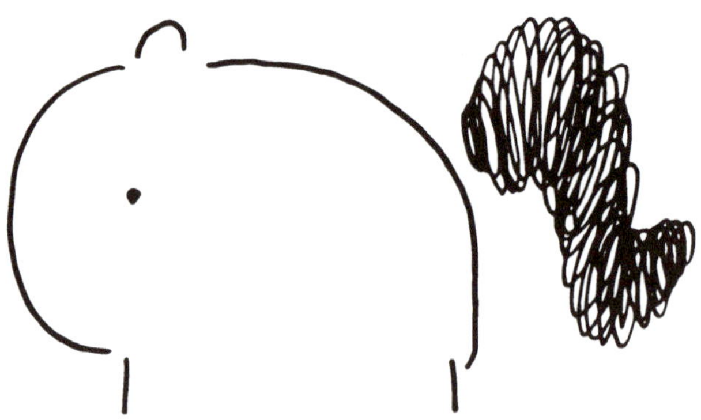

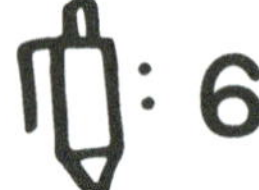

Beaver

wood-eating flat-tailed big mouse

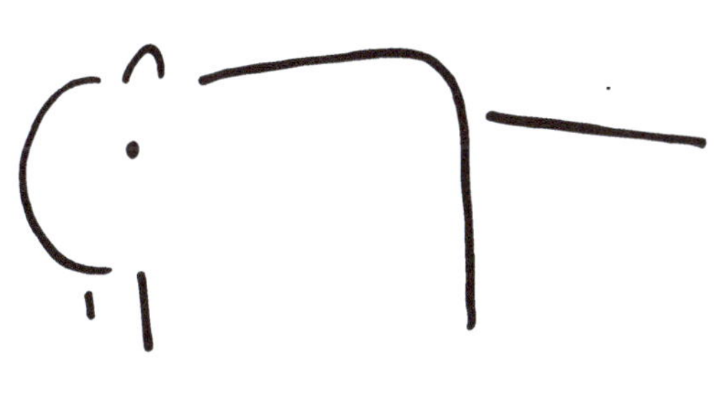

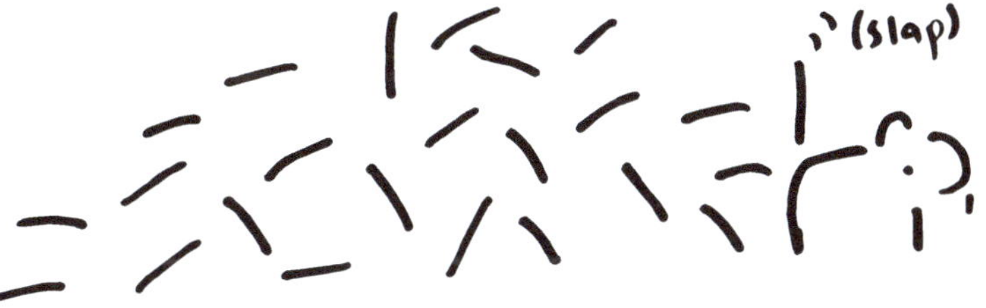

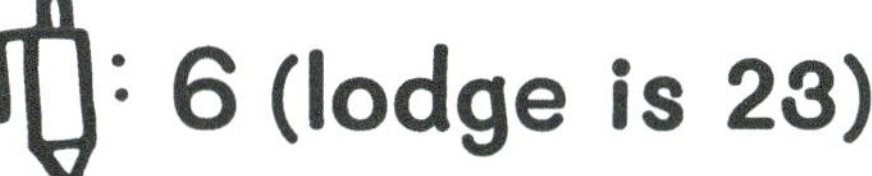

Bat

mouse with wings

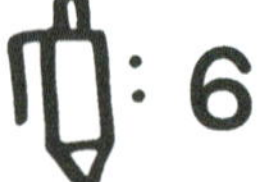
: 6

Weasel

furry snake with legs

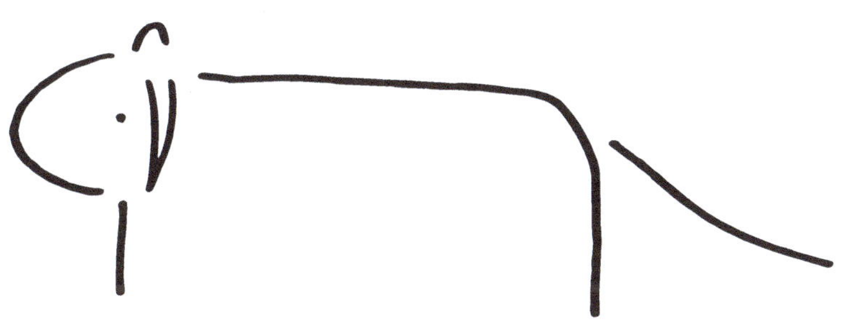

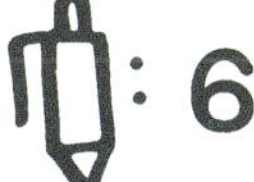

Otter

swimming weasel

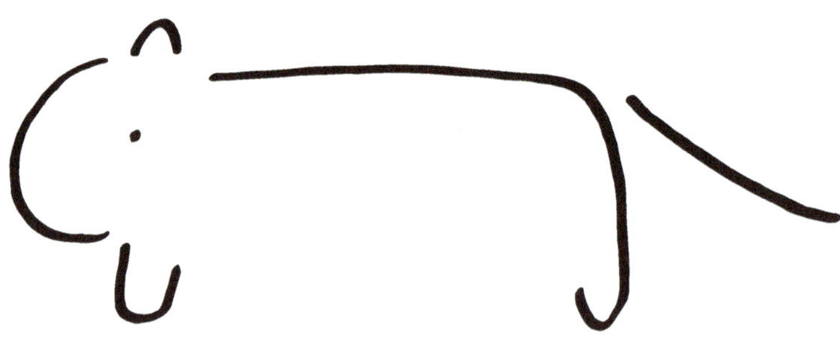

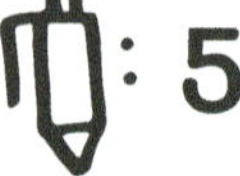
: 5

Platypus

otter with a duck bill

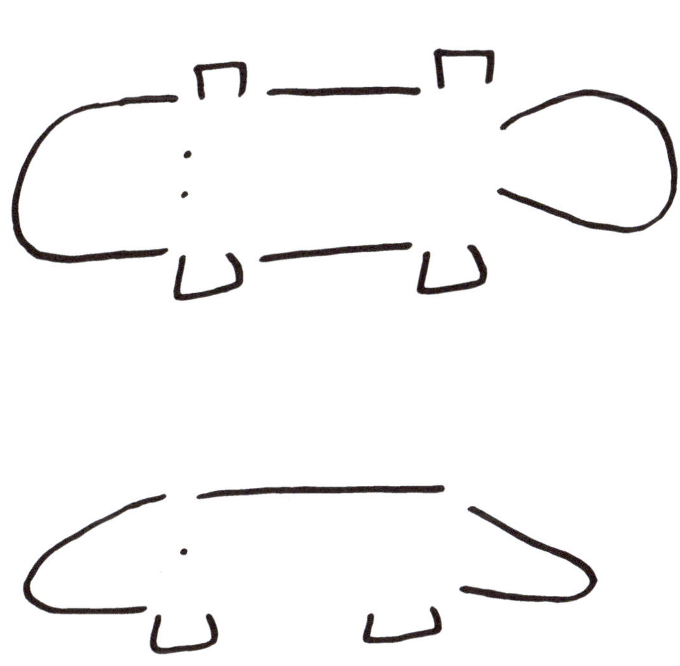

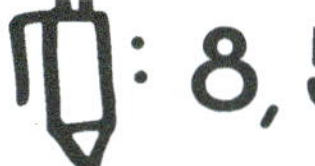

: 8, 5

Armadillo

mouse with a shell

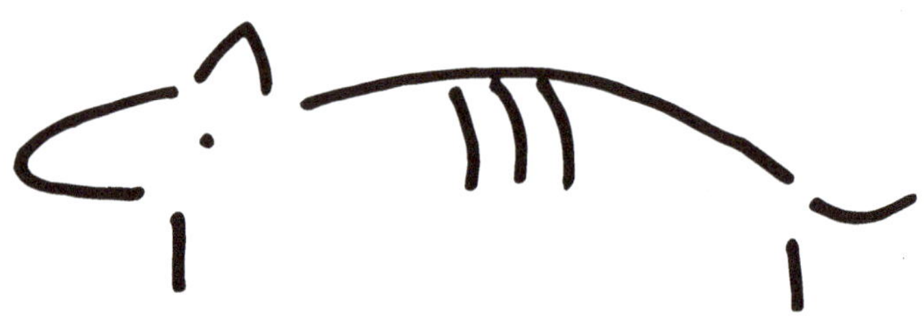

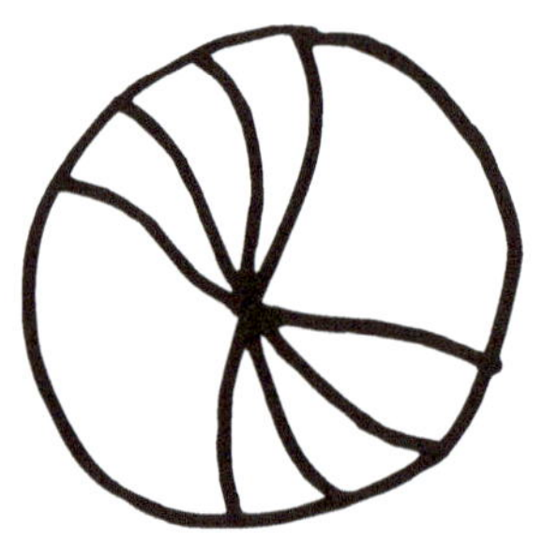

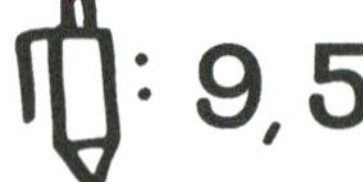

Mole

mouse with a weird nose
and it digs

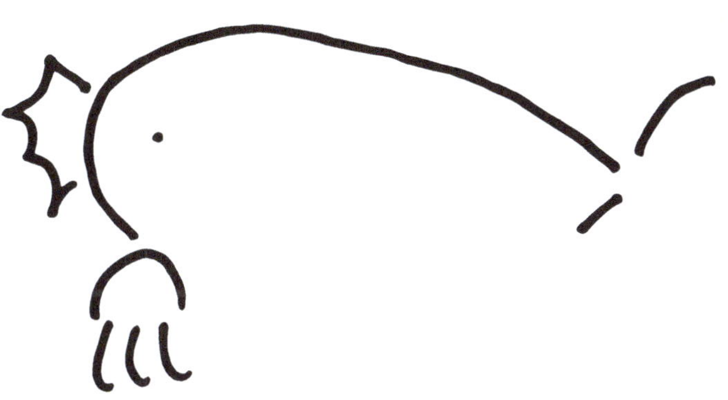

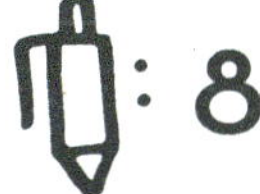
: 8

Kangaroo

huge mutant rabbit

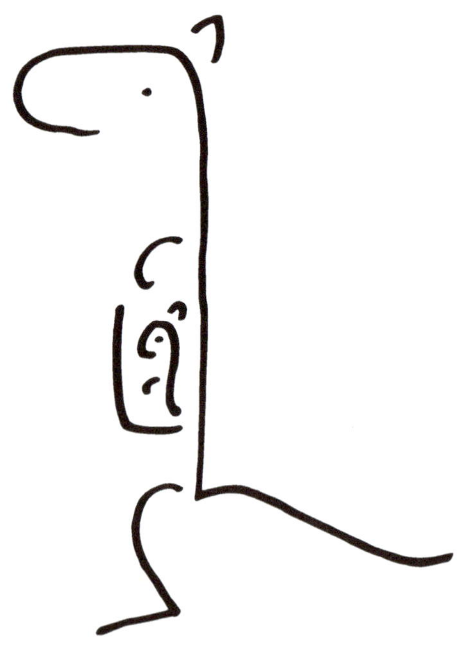

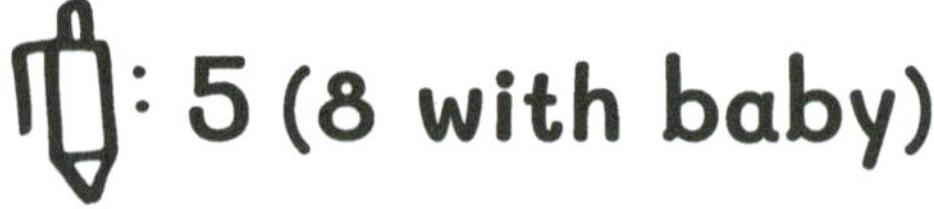

Koala

tiny bear in a tree

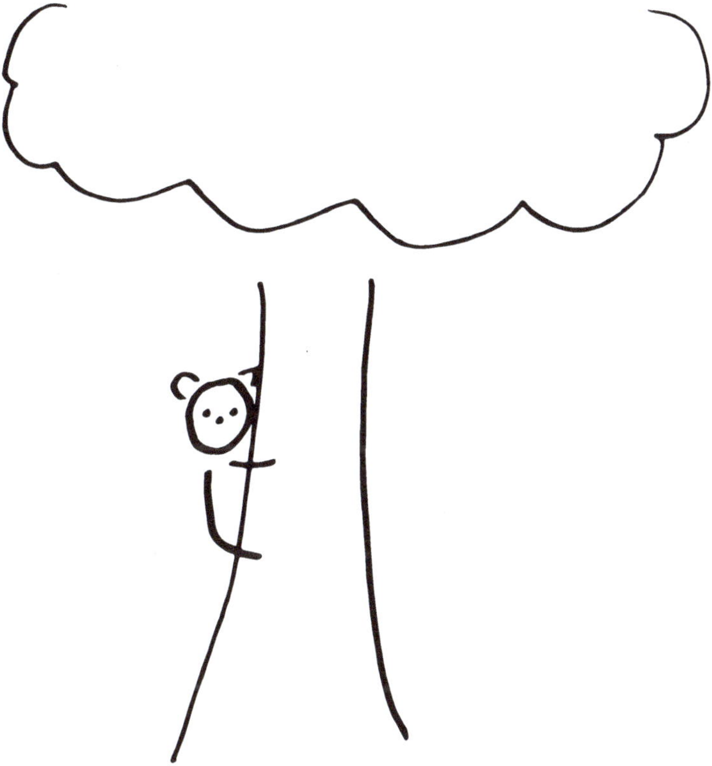

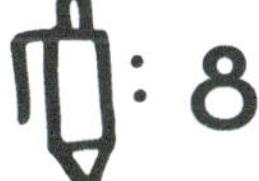

Sloth

really slow monkey

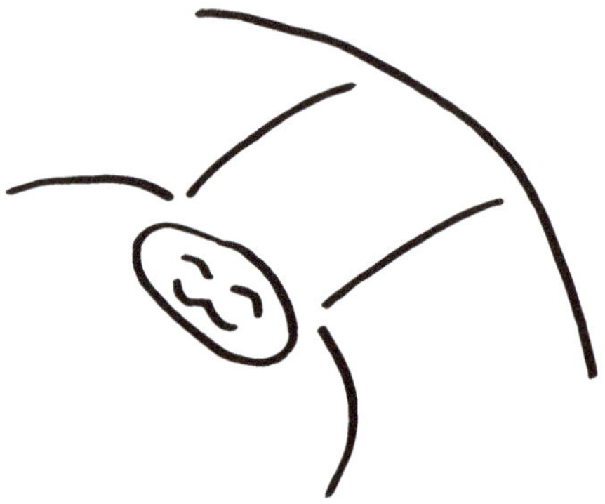

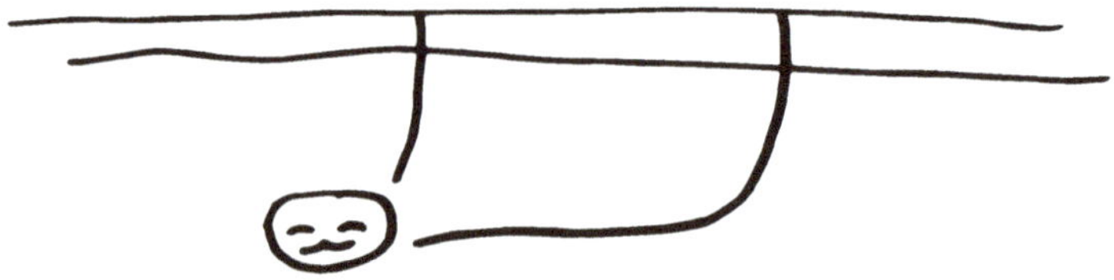

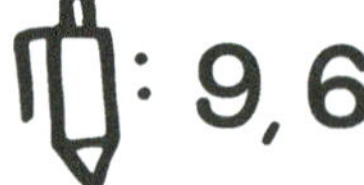

Porcupine & Hedgehog

(big) spiky hamster

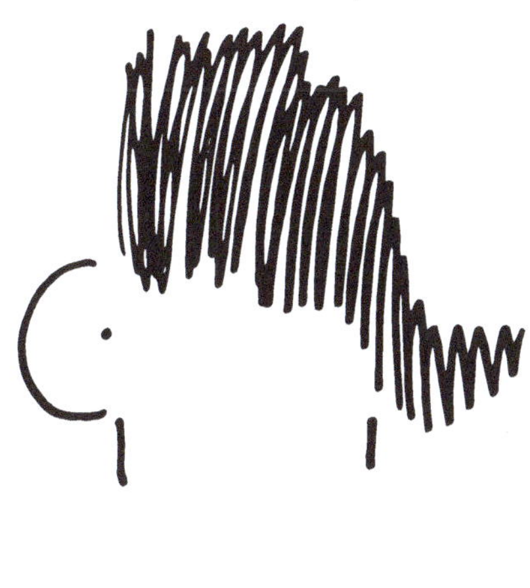

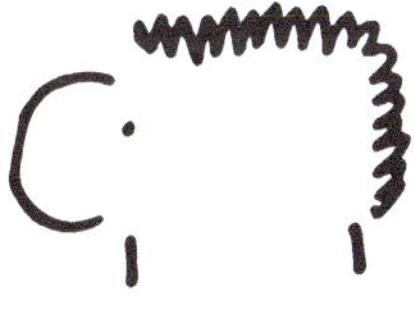

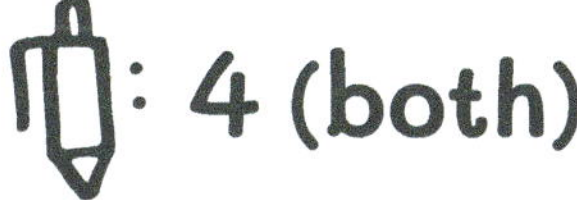

Assorted insects and such

Butterfly, Spider, Mantis, Scorpion, Fly, Bee, Mosquito, Caterpillar

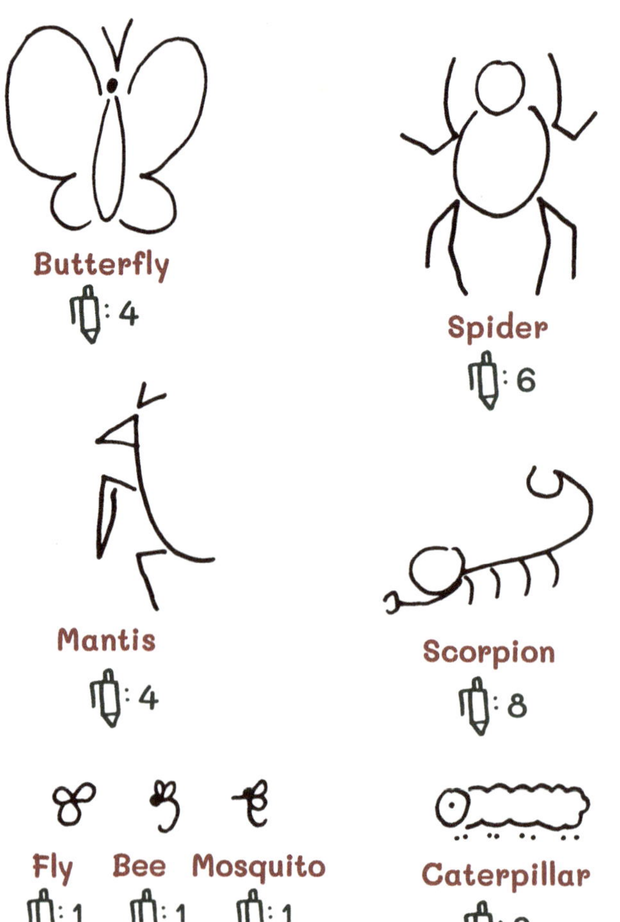

Snail

rock-house slime thing

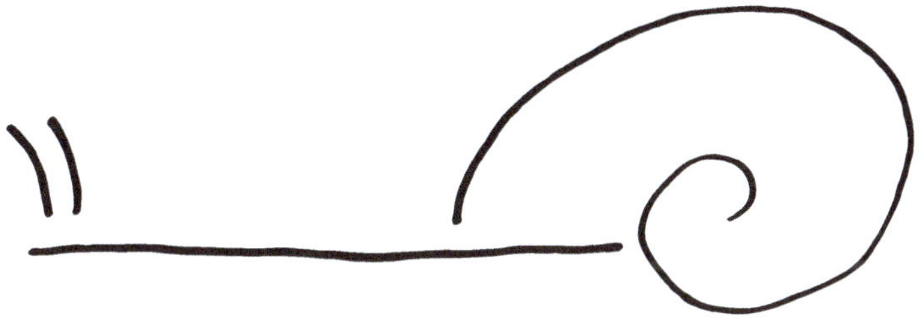

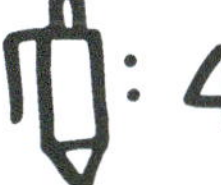

Parrot

loud rainbow pet bird

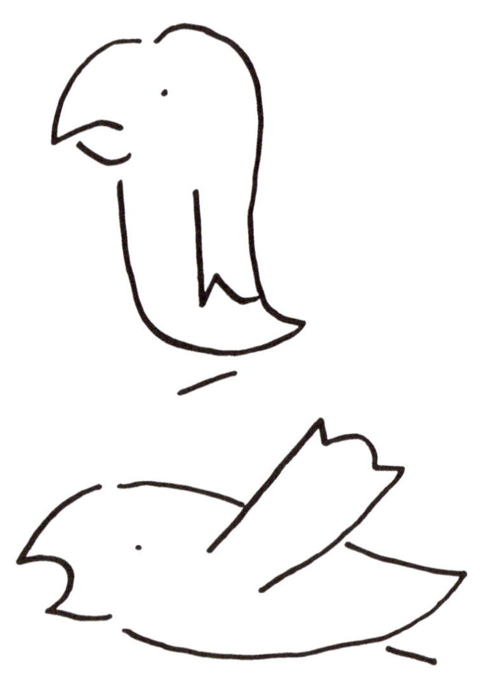

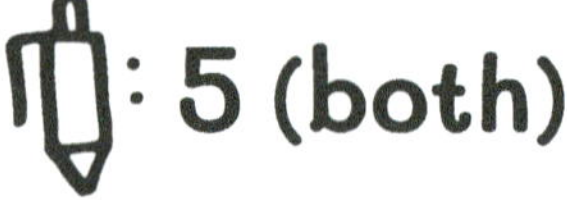

Penguin

black & white flightless bird

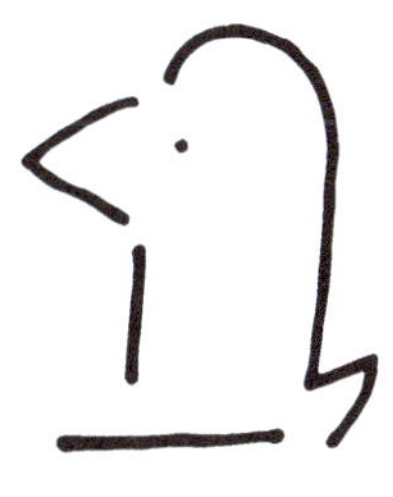

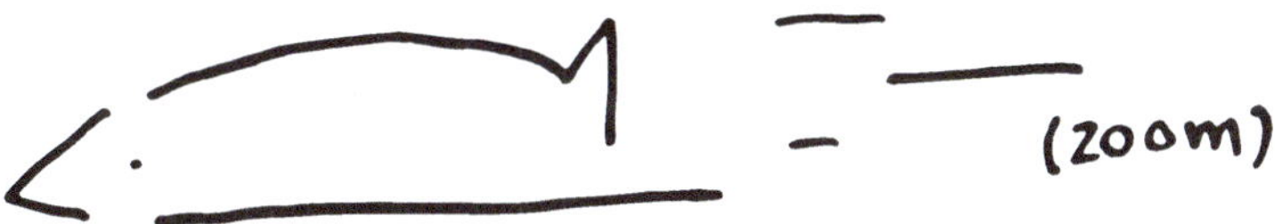

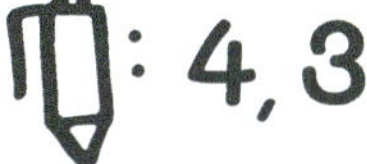

Owl

big-eyed fat bird

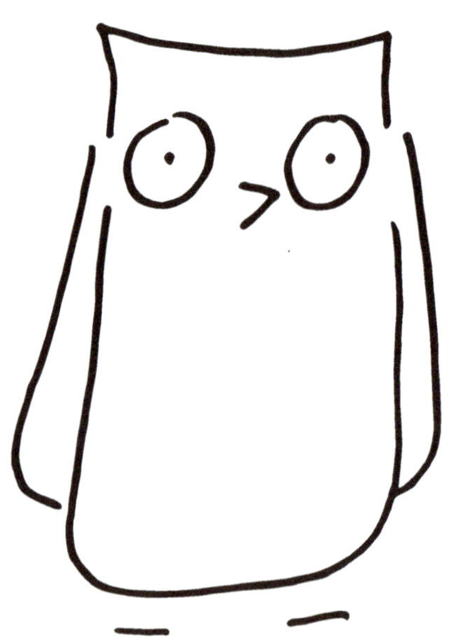

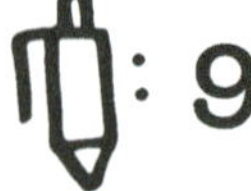

Ostrich

tall goose

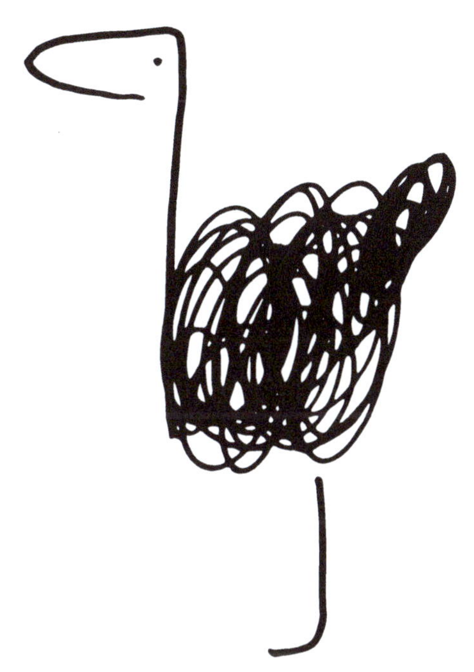

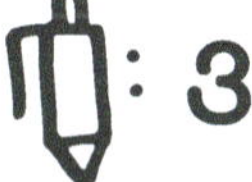

Pterodactyl

big, birdlike flying lizard

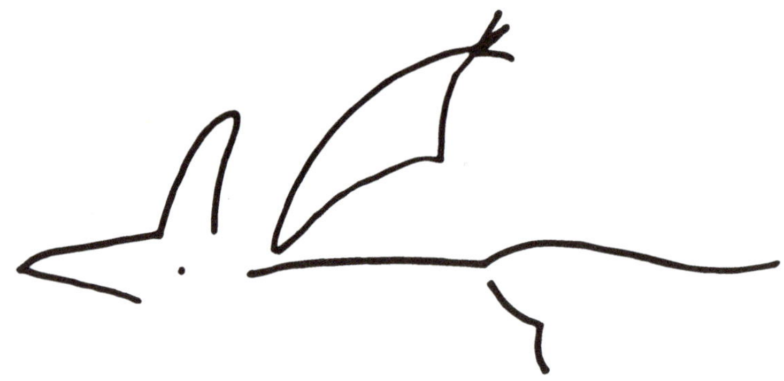

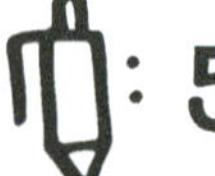
: 5

T. Rex

huge, upright lizard with teeth

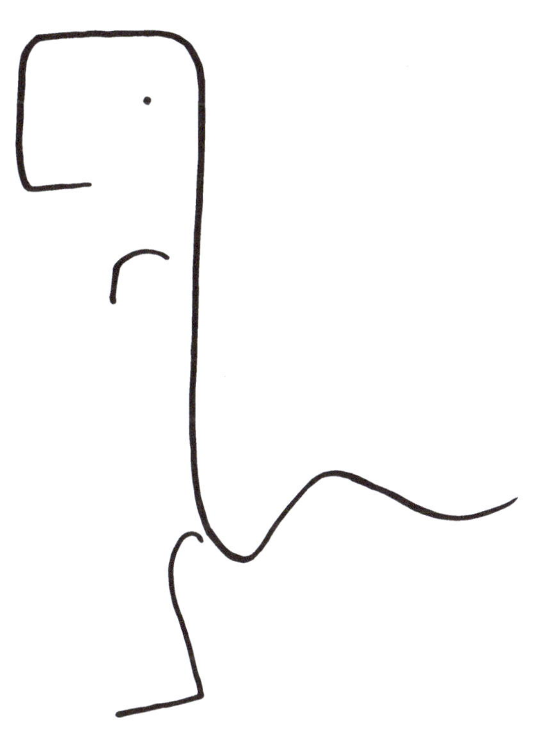

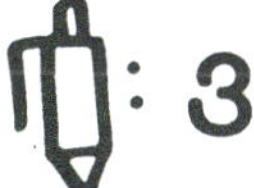

Plesiosaur

long, seallike water lizard

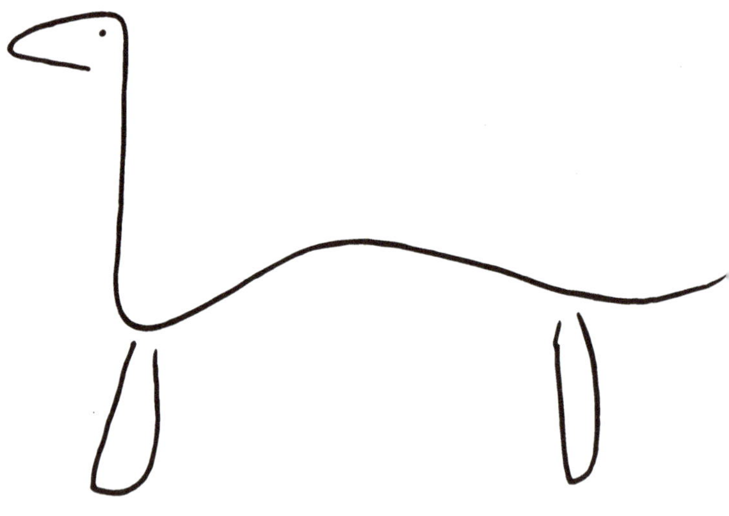

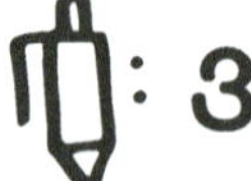

Stegosaurus

big lizard with spines

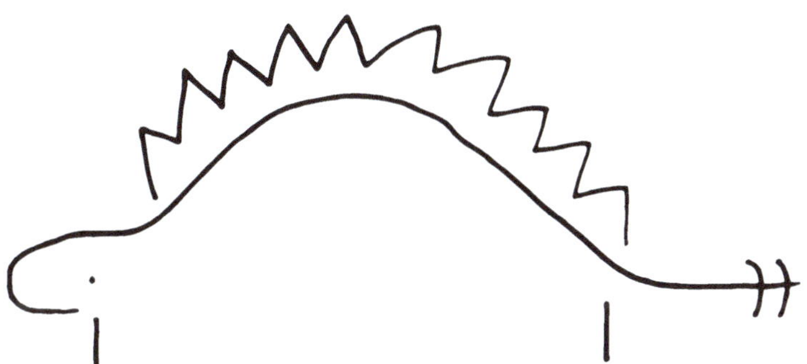

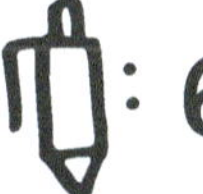

Brachiosaurus
(or any other like this)

huge tall long lizard

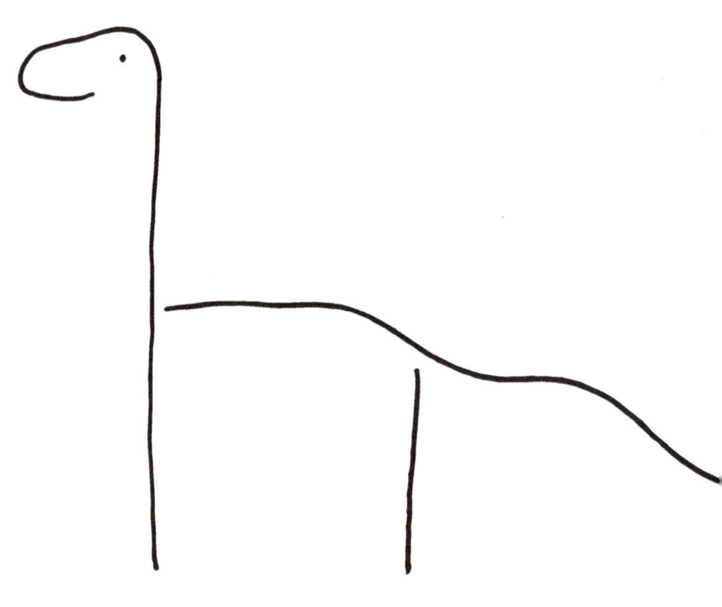

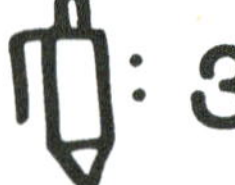

: 3

Dimetrodon

big lizard with a frill on
its back

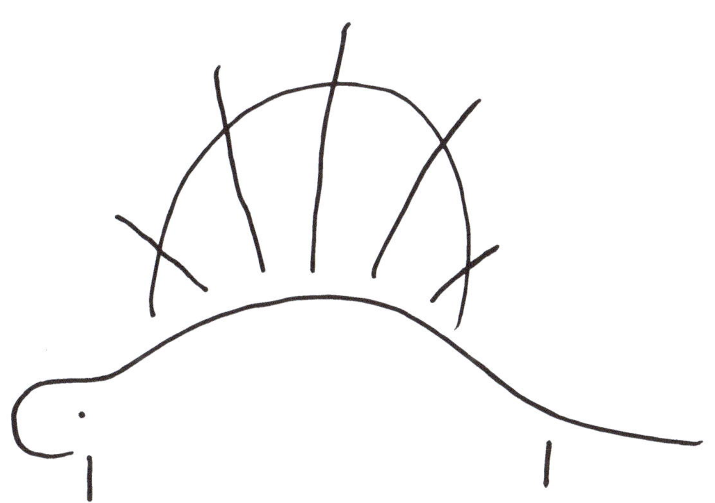

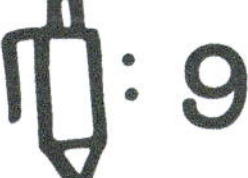

Unicorn

horse with a big horn

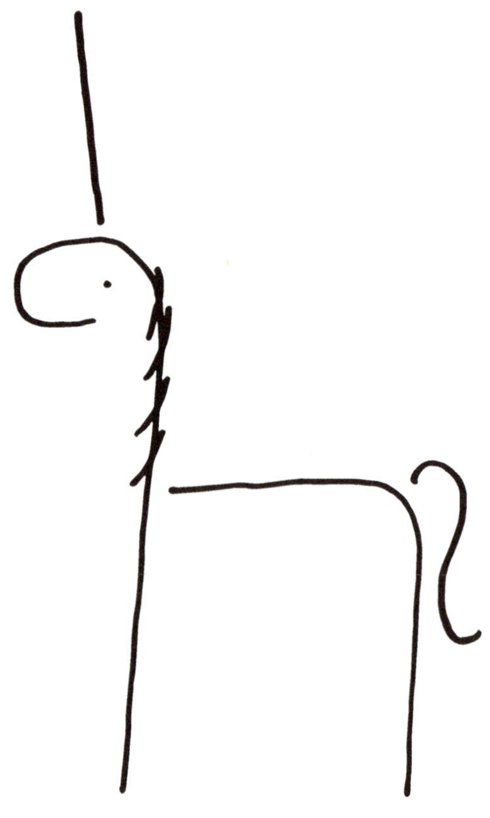

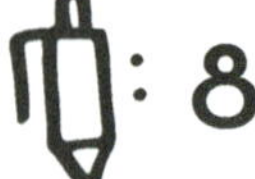

Dragon

giant flying lizard with crazy breath

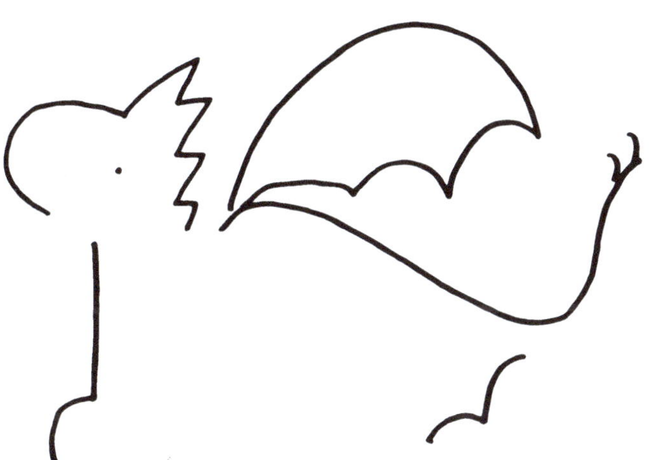

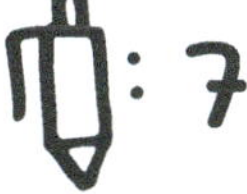

CPSIA information can be obtained
at www.ICGtesting.com
Printed in the USA
LVHW072356150120
643781LV00001B/1